First published in 2021 by Wayland
Text copyright © Pat Thomas 2021
Illustrations copyright © Hodder and Stoughton 2021

Wayland, an imprint of Hachette Children's Group
Part of Hodder and Stoughton
Carmelite House
50 Victoria Embankment
London EC4Y 0DZ

First edition for the United States and Canada
published in 2021 by B.E.S. Publishing.

All inquiries should be addressed to:
Peterson's Publishing
4380 S. Syracuse Street, Suite 200
Denver, CO 80237–2624
www.petersonsbooks.com

ISBN: 978-1-4380-8967-6

Printed in China
9 8 7 6 5 4 3 2 1

FSC
www.fsc.org

MISTO
Carta da fonti gestite
in maniera responsabile
FSC® C144853

SOMETIMES STOPPING IS HARD

A FIRST LOOK AT ADDICTION

Written by
PAT THOMAS

B.E.S. PUBLISHING

Illustrated by
CLARE KEAY

Nobody's perfect.

From time to time, we
all make mistakes
and bad choices.

We can hurt other people's feelings even if we don't mean to. That's just part of being human.

The important thing is that
we learn from our mistakes.

Mistakes can teach us
what not to do. They teach
us what works better
and what makes us,
and the people we
love, feel better.

But some people find it hard to learn.
They keep doing things that are bad for them.

When you just can't stop doing something even if it is really bad for you, that's called addiction.

People can become addicted to lots of different things. Most often it is drugs and alcohol.

But people can also become addicted to other things too, such as gambling or shopping.

WHAT ABOUT YOU?

Does someone close to you have an addiction?
What does that mean to you?

When you have an addiction, it can
be hard to think about anything else.

It can hurt your health. It can hurt relationships
with people you care about and who care about
you. It can make it hard to get and keep a job.

It's hard to understand why people keep
doing things that are bad for them.
Sometimes it's because they are
sad, afraid, or in pain.
They may feel like
they have no
other choices.

People with an addiction use alcohol and drugs as a way of forgetting about their problems for a while.

But it doesn't make those problems go away—and most often it makes them worse.

When one person in a family has an addiction it affects everyone else.

It can make them forget to do things. It can make them angry one minute and happy the next. It can make them unpredictable and unreliable.

17

If someone you care about has an addiction, it's normal to feel scared, angry, or confused—or just very sad.

It's normal to worry that it's somehow your fault and feel that you want to help.

But it's never your fault if someone you love
has an addiction. And it's not your job to fix it either.

WHAT ABOUT YOU?

Do you sometimes feel that it's your fault
if someone you love has an addiction?
Do you try to fix things? If so, how?

Maybe you have seen someone in your family making bad choices or hanging out with others who are making bad choices.

Seeing people you care about make bad choices that could turn into an addiction can make you feel helpless.

It's painful when someone who is older than you, or someone you look up to, keeps making bad decisions.

If someone in your family is addicted to drugs or alcohol, you might worry that you will grow up to be that way, too.

But you don't have to make the same choices that others do. We can all find healthier, happier ways to live.

Most people with addictions do want to stop.
But they need help and support to do that.
They may need that help and support
for the rest of their lives.

But living with someone who has an addiction is hard, so their friends and family need help and support, too.

It's important to have people who you trust to talk to and share your feelings with. You should always tell someone you trust if you are feeling scared or unsafe.

WHAT ABOUT YOU?

Who helps you?
Is there someone you trust who you can talk to?

People with an addiction
have to want to help
themselves in order
to get well.

No one else can solve
their problems for them.

When someone you love is really trying
to get better, it will mean a lot if you show that
you care about them and cheer them on when
they are making better choices.

WELL DONE!
WE LOVE YOU,
CONGRATS, MOM!

HOW TO USE THIS BOOK

Addiction is a complex and emotive subject. It can take a long time to talk through all there is to say about it. This book is aimed at helping to open up first discussions with young children and is meant to be read with children as a way of encouraging them to be active partners in the discussion. Try reading the book first and familiarizing yourself with its content before you begin. The "What about you?" questions throughout the text can be useful prompts for understanding things from your child's point of view. You may find benefit in reading the book with your child more than once. Repetition allows young children to formulate thoughts and questions as the need arises.

When you are ready to talk to a child about addiction consider the following points:

Start with the familiar. With young children who are still very "me" focused, concrete discussions about someone you know or someone you have seen who is struggling with addiction may be more productive than more abstract discussions about "other people."

Be honest. Use real words, not euphemisms. Explain clearly and simply that an addiction means a person finds it hard to stop using drugs or alcohol. Help the child understand that addiction is an illness that has many causes including mental illness, a traumatic experience in the past, growing up in a damaging environment, or even genetic reasons.

Provide reassurance. If the child you are reading with has a family member struggling with addiction, it is important to reassure them that they are not to blame and that it is not their job to fix things.

Help them understand that when a person is in the grip of an addiction they may do things that they would never normally do and may say things they don't mean. This includes breaking promises, saying mean things, ignoring them, hurting themselves or others, disappearing for periods, or even falling asleep at unusual times.

Provide support. Children living with family members who have an addiction need both practical and emotional support. Support organizations, networks and forums, teachers and sports coaches, church groups, other family members, and friends can all help a child feel less alone, upset, or scared.

Keep the lines of communication open—but try not to lecture. Take advantage of opportunities that arise naturally to speak to your child about issues like substance abuse and addiction. Let them know that their feelings, thoughts, and opinions are important. Use experiences from your own life to talk about the challenges with peer pressure and how you coped with it. Remember also to keep things in perspective: most of their peers are unlikely to be using drugs or alcohol.

Avoid value judgements. Avoid framing discussions in terms of right or wrong. Remember that children love their parents (even if they've said or done terrible things). Helping kids separate the parent from the behavior acknowledges the love children feel for their parents, but allows them to share their feelings about the addiction.

Schools can help. Teachers are ideally placed to open discussions with young children about their bodies and the things they need to stay healthy, as well as the things that harm health.

These kinds of lessons fall under a broad heading of encouraging "health esteem" and can be used to help children set goals and aspirations for a healthy body and mind now and in the future. Class projects, drawing and writing activities, quizzes, and role playing can help children identify those activities that enhance health and those that harm it as well as understand the risks of certain behaviors such as smoking, drugs, and alcohol consumption and explain how harmful substances can "play tricks" with your brain to make you think they are good for you. Lessons should reinforce the idea that we all have rights and responsibilities to maintain good health, help children to recognize the risks and safety rules in relation to medicines and household products and provide strategies for not falling victim to peer pressure.

FURTHER READING

Wishes and Worries: Coping with a Parent Who Drinks Too Much Alcohol
Centre for Addiction and Mental Health
(Tundra Books, 2011)

Mommy's Disease: Helping Children Understand Alcoholism
Carolyn Hannan Bell (CreateSpace Independent Publishing Platform, 2014)

Daddy's Disease (Helping Children Understand)
Carolyn Hannan Bell (CreateSpace Independent Publishing Platform, 2013)

My Dad Loves Me, My Dad Has a Disease: A Child's View: Living With Addiction
Claudia Black (MAC Publishing, 1997)

My Big Sister Takes Drugs by Judith Vigna
(Albert Whitman & Company, 1995)

Critters Cry Too: Explaining Addiction to Children
Anthuny Curcio (ICG Children's, 2016)

An Elephant in the Living Room
M. Hastings and Marion H. Typpo (Hazelden Publishing, 1994)

USEFUL WEBSITES

Substance Abuse and Mental Health Services Administration
https://www.samhsa.gov/find-help/national-helpline

American Addiction Centers
https://www.projectknow.com/support-groups/families-of-addicts/

Hazelden Betty Ford Foundation
https://www.hazeldenbettyford.org/treatment/family-children/childrens-program

National Association for Children of Addiction
https://nacoa.org/